A CHILD'S BOOK OF MANNERS

written by Ruth Shannon Odor

illustrated by Joanne (Jodie) McCallum

Library of Congress Catalog Card Number 89-52030
©1990, The STANDARD PUBLISHING Company, Cincinnati, Ohio
Division of STANDEX INTERNATIONAL Corporation. Printed in U.S.A.

Good manners are just being kind and thinking of others.

From early in the morning till the end of day,

do and say the kindest things in the
kindest way.

Good manners begin at home.

Close doors
quietly.

Walk—do not run—
in the house.

Hang up your clothes.

Put toys away.

At the table, don't talk with your mouth full.

If you want to leave the table, ask, "May I be excused?"
If Mother or Father says, "Yes," answer, "Thank you".

Don't be . . .

A "Shoveler" Shawn

A "Picky" Pete

A Susie "the Slurper"

A "Messy" Bessy

Cover your mouth . . .

when you cough,

when you yawn,

when you sneeze.

Walk—do not run—in the halls.
Never push or shove.
Help take care of the building
and the playground.

There are some very special rules
to follow when you go to school.

Say *please* if you want something.

Say *thank you* when you are
given something.

Say *no, thank you* when you
do not want something.

Friends don't just happen. If you
want a friend, you have to be one.

Take turns.

Share.

Play fair.

Don't be like . . .

"Sulky" Sue

"Me–first" Megan

"Look–at–me" Louie

"That's mine" Tracy

Follow the rules.

Take turns.

Be a good loser.

Play fair.

Be kind. Do not make fun of others. Do not brag—even if you *are* the best.

Be honest. Copying the
answers may be the easy way,
but it is not God's way.

Always tell the truth—even
when it is not easy.

When you go to church, try to be early. If you *are* late, sit near the back.

Do not whisper or giggle or talk. Do not rattle the pages of the songbook. When you disturb others, they cannot worship God.

Do not read your story paper—
wait until you are home. Listen
to God's Word.

Think about God. Sing to God.
Pray to God. Listen to God.

Jesus taught us . . .
        to be kind,
        to love others,
        to treat others as we
    would like to be treated.

Jesus is God's Son. Jesus
loves others more than himself.

If we try to be like Jesus in all
we say and do, then having good
manners will be as easy as . . .